Praise for *It's About Time*

"In the digital age, there's more on our plates than ever, coming from every direction from print to tweets, to pings and rings. Shannon and Shawn have nailed the reason why we are more distracted from *the* most important productivity tasks and have provided the most tangible ways to solve these problems."
--Mario M. Martinez, Jr., CEO, Founder & Digital Sales Evangelist, Vengreso

"As the CEO of a major digital marketing company, and owner of multiple businesses, my time is valuable. This book is a wonderful resource and probably has the most genius name for a book. Ever. Read it!"
--Jason Anthony, CEO, Jason Anthony Group

"It's About Time is the right book at the right time; in our ever-connected world, there never seems to be enough time! My company was founded on the ideals of using technology to improve process and automation. The authors have captured common-sense, no-nonsense tips on how to approach your life with a productive lens."
--Harbinder Khera, CEO, Mindmatrix

"I always look for ways to stay relevant and maximize productivity. This book reminds us that we need to manage our time successfully. As the CEO of a successful technology company, I find this book to be a great tool for all busy professionals."
--Ted Teele, CEO, Touchtown

"There are many demands on my time as CEO of a rapid-paced business consulting firm. *It's About Time* is an insightful guide to help keep my priorities aligned so I can focus on delivering strategic value to my clients."
--Denise DeSimone, CEO, C-leveled

"Time management is such an important skill for anyone serious about running a business. McBride and Gregg have constructed the how-to manual for improving your time management with practical real-world executables that anyone can implement quickly. This one should be kept close and re-read on occasion to keep the skills sharp. Well done!"
--Jim Whipp, CEO, St. Agnes Federal Credit Union

"Time is our most important and scarce resource; it brings us memories, great times, laughter, and tears, and once it's gone, it's gone. *It's About Time* is a great resource for all of us wanting to make the most out of our time to do the most good. As the leader of my company, working to prioritize clients, family, friends, and life, this is a great book to keep handy!"
--Dionne Mischler, CEO, Inside Sales by Design

"Life happens to all of us! Space on the calendar doesn't magically open and in my world of PhD studies and the brave entry into entrepreneurship, it has become critical that my time, energy and resources are maximized. Productivity and prioritization are a way of life! And, that's why the timeliness of this book is so critical. If you want to work at your highest level and this book is in your hands, you've landed in the right spot."
--Atiya Abdelmalik, MSN, RN, CEO, Author,
Leading with Wellbeing coach

"As business owners and moms, we recognize how important time management is. In today's world where women have to handle their careers and families, it becomes extremely difficult to find the time to get everything done on your long list of never-ending things to do. This book could not have come at a better time. It's a must-read for all working parents struggling to keep up with the everyday demands of life."
--Kimberly Kirsch Soder and Heather Kirsch Petz
CEO/President, Champion Cheer Central

IT'S ABOUT TIME

How to Do More
of What Matters
in the Time You Have

R. Shawn McBride & Shannon J. Gregg

This book is dedicated to those who are on their way to getting things done. So often in society we hear, "There's just not enough time." We all have time, and this book is dedicated to those on the path to making great use of *their* time.

". . . little by little, you will see your way. I mean in every sense, your way in life and in thinking. It may be uphill pedalling at first."
                    -- James Joyce, *Portrait of the Artist as a Young Man*

ISBN: 978-1-945605-01-7

Illustrations by Blake Kandzer
Kandzer Design, www.kandzer.com

Disclaimer: The information and ideas presented in this book are for educational purposes only. No attorney-client relationship is formed by the use of this book, and this book does not constitute legal advice. This book is not intended to be a substitute for consulting with a qualified attorney. You should consult an attorney of your choice to discuss and implement your particular legal strategies. The authors and publisher disclaim any liability arising directly or indirectly from this book.

Foreword

Introduction

Part One: Time Management

Part Two: Productivity

Conclusion

Acknowledgments

About the Authors

Worksheet

Foreword

I am the COO of a startup maker business, a full-time project manager for a graphics company, a professional photographer, a mom and wife. In all those roles, the most daunting thing to learn is time management and the discipline of good productivity. I'm not more naturally equipped at doing it than the next guy, but I understand the need to always be learning how to improve myself and my skills.

Filtering through all the talking heads on YouTube and television barking about how "You can make a million dollars," can be desensitizing and make it difficult to know who is worth your time to take advice from. I look to the people in my life who are achieving their goals and I talk with them about how they are doing that. One of the people I rely on is Shannon J. Gregg. Her education and experience make me confident that she provides solid advice. She zooms into a problem and offers sound critiques and wisdom on how to navigate through it. Our business talks always result in great solutions and even more meaningful goals.

The other dependable voice is R. Shawn McBride, whom I have learned a lot from through his online tools and videos. Shawn has a proven record in helping businesses and individuals attain their goals and provides a great deal of insight into how average workers can use the same tools as an executive-level manager to make their lives easier and find more success in a shorter amount of time.

It is a daily tightrope walk to have to navigate where to focus my attention. Between a day job, to managing a small business, to staying educated, as well as all of the normal familial commitments that I have, it can become overwhelming without the right tools. Actually, time management was probably one of the biggest factors that held me back from taking on new roles in my career or in starting a new business sooner. Shannon helped to pull back the curtain a bit to show me that I could be great at all of the things I wanted to do and still have my sanity at the end of the day.

Token ideas about time management and productivity can seem very common sense to most people, but just because it seems to be common sense doesn't mean the best methodology comes naturally to everyone. If that were true, there would be no need for all of the thousands of books written on the subject to exist. Along with that point, sometimes even the most effective people need to center themselves back to basics in order to grow.

Perhaps you don't need to be reminded to stay focused, but you do need to refresh yourself on how to make a plan for a new opportunity. I am a careful planner, but I'm also very sensitive; when a plan deviates from what I had intended I can sometimes find myself spinning and feeling overwhelmed. I will sometimes need to remind myself that with a calm head I make better decisions.

Sometimes a plan has to be flexible and I may not always have built in a fluid adjustment to a deviation. That doesn't make me a failure but it does require me to stop and center myself so I can work out the problem. Recognizing where I struggle has helped me to avoid those panic points and quickly adjust for them. The building blocks of how to be more effective in your life are exactly what this guide is about.

Thanks to Shannon's and Shawn's insights and experiences, the following read is conversational and allows any reader to understand and digest how each point is applicable to any given situation. As you read, think about your experiences that have either utilized these techniques or how these tips could have been useful at the time. Remember, no one is an expert at everything and it takes a lot of different viewpoints to build an expert at anything.

--Heidi Jacobs, COO, Slap Stuff Together

Introduction

Best recipes for 30-minute meals.
The 7-minute workout to get in shape fast.
How to fall asleep in 60 seconds.

If you have time to browse the internet for time-saving solutions, your search engine has spewed out countless websites. We buy magazines devoted to simplifying our lives, come up with ten questions for three-minute speed-dating sessions, and eat an apple and microwave popcorn for lunch at our desks. The issue is critical: Time management.

The marketing that comes at us incessantly and the stress that we feel regularly make it seem that time is an issue specific to now, but it is not.

With the development of cuneiform writing in about 4000 B.C., the Mesopotamians gave us the first to-do lists. What were the time concerns about 500 years later when the Egyptians used a tall obelisk to track shadows created by the sun? Fast-forward to the 18th century A.D., as farmers rushed to harvest crops, Benjamin Franklin noted that time is money. The pace of innovation propels us and is partly responsible for today's struggle to juggle family, work, friends, leisure – all the pieces of life.

We all have 168 hours in a week, and we have at least some control over how we spend them. We must rest, or our bodies will shut down. If we get the often-eluded eight hours of sleep a night, that leaves us with 112 hours in the week. To shower. To eat. To commute to the full-time job that is billed as a 40-hour work week but often runs longer. To get to the grocery store. To get the kids to soccer practices. To cheer at the kids' soccer games. To hop on the treadmill. To attend the work conference a three-hour flight away. There's the dentist's appointment, the car needs an oil change, and the lawn needs to be mowed. Our time is whittling down.

Who doesn't wish we had more time? But there's a difference between needing more time and making the most of the time we have.

Set aside time to read this book.

In the first section, R. Shawn McBride takes on time management, drawing from his experiences as a lawyer and entrepreneur. Then, Shannon J. Gregg, MBA, a sales productivity expert, calls attention to ways to be more productive with your time.

The authors have spent years working their businesses, growing with competing demands, and helping others execute plans and find ways to do more in less time. They will challenge you and give you tools to manage your time and be more productive.

Use the worksheet at the end of this book to record your thoughts as you read.

There is no quick solution, but there is a real solution so that you will have more time.

Part One

Time Management

1. Plan

Somewhere, sometime, someone probably told you to write down your goals. The much-ballyhooed theory is that people who put their goals in writing are more likely to achieve them. Seems obvious, then, that the same must hold true for time management. People who have a written plan for their time must be able to better manage what needs to be done, and so they get more done, right?

Let's take a look.

You may have heard of a famous study conducted by an Ivy League college in the 1950s, where graduating seniors were asked to write down their goals. Two decades later, a follow-up study revealed that the graduates who put their goals in writing had accomplished so much more than those who hadn't bothered to list their aspirations. How much more? The 3% who wrote down their goals were earning ten times more than the others combined. The findings of that 1953 Harvard study were fantastic. Or was it a 1953 Yale study?

There's the problem.

Turns out there was no Harvard or Yale study that looked into what happens when a 20-something puts goals in writing. No study at all on this topic from the 1950s. It's a myth, with the lesson repeated and repeated and repeated by life coaches, motivational speakers, bosses, teachers and New Year's resolution-makers.

So, for a while, we were uncertain whether there were benefits to written plans. Then a psychology professor at Dominican University of California set out to learn if there were any validity to this decades-old myth that, by the way, appears to have an unknown origin.

Professor Gail Matthews recruited participants with a variety of professions -- from entrepreneurs to artists -- and randomly assigned them to one of five groups. Participants in one group were instructed to simply think about and rate their goals, with the other groups' tasks growing more complex until the fifth group was asked to formulate action commitments and send their goals and weekly progress reports to supportive friends. The participants' goals varied, with the most popular being "complete a project" such as hiring employees, updating a website and writing a chapter of a book. After four weeks, participants rated themselves on their progress.

And that is how we finally have a study demonstrating empirical evidence that writing down your goal enhances your chances for achievement.

At the end of the study, only 43 percent of those who didn't write down their goals said they either had accomplished their goal or were at least half-way there. But among those who wrote down their goals, shared their commitment and progress reports with a supportive friend, the success rate jumped to 76 percent

Those who write things down and are focused will accomplish more in life.

For those of us trying to manage time, a written plan or at least a very strong concept of our plan allows us to tackle what we really want to get done.

A key to being an effective time manager is to know what you want to accomplish and put it in writing. Use your written word as a map to determine what to focus on and how to allocate your time. Everything will build from a plan. Tie your plans to your goals. Know where you are going in life. That knowledge and your map will allow you to do more to accomplish your goals.

Step away from the hustle and bustle.

Stop listening to those who tell you to follow a standard career path or to do certain things a certain way. Figure out your priorities.

When you start with a written plan, it becomes easier to determine where to focus and how to spend your time.

2. Pay Attention

On an especially hectic day, life in a little house on the prairie in 1870 might seem appealing. Snowed in by a blizzard, reading and quilting and whittling by candlelight, oblivious to life beyond the four log walls.

But could you do it for long, really? You don't have to go back a century-and-a-half -- how about a decade?

The world has changed so much in such a short time that many of us cannot imagine life without our Facebook walls, Twitter feeds, Instagram posts, emails and texts in whatever combination we choose from the many options to stay informed and connected. Sometimes we even use our cell phones to talk to another person. We can turn to our smartphones to reply to emails, read last night's box scores and today's headlines, text friends, watch a movie, whatever our priorities or distractions are at that moment -- while attending a business meeting, sitting at a red light, or jogging on the treadmill.

We multitask. We attempt to do several things at once, usually relying on as many technologies as possible. Common sense tells us something gets short-changed when we multitask. So we can be pretty mediocre at a lot of things all at the same time.

In his book *CrazyBusy*, Dr. Edward Hallowell calls multitasking "a mythical activity." He is a psychiatrist who specializes in the treatment of attention deficit hyperactivity disorder. He coined the term "attention deficit trait" to describe the condition he estimates at least half of us in today's workplace feel -- overwhelmed, distracted, and pulled off course.

Researchers at the University of California Irvine studied interruptions among office workers. Led by Gloria Mark, a professor in the Department of Informatics, the researchers found workers who were interrupted by a phone call or email took an average 25 minutes to return to their original task. Although other studies have found interruptions can be both beneficial and detrimental, the UC Irvine researchers concluded that people compensate for interruptions by working faster. But they pay for it with more stress, higher frustrations, effort and time pressure.

The scientific literature is filled with studies that look at our attention and interruptions. Though we know our need to focus at work isn't a life-or-death situation for most of us -- we're not all nurses and pilots -- it is an issue. Back in 2005, Basex authors took the first in-depth look at how much interruptions such as instant messages, the web and spam emails cost U.S. businesses. Their conclusion: 28 billion lost hours annually, worth $588 billion. No way that amount is less today.

When we talk about multitasking, we are talking about paying attention. We gain a competitive advantage by learning to focus on the task at hand. Keep your attention on one task for a specific period – ignoring all that technology tempts us with every second. That keeps you on the path to accomplish your goal.

3. Remain Calm

"I'm stressed out."

We hear others say it. We say it.

We appreciate that the stress spectrum is long and that the trigger one day may be inconsequential the next. But in a discussion about time management, the stress usually can be traced to too many demands, too much to do, and too little time.

On top of that, there's a constant influx of information and communication. If someone wants this author's attention, the contact options include telephone, email, text, LinkedIn, Facebook, Twitter, and a blog page. That's at the moment this is written. The number of ways for contact and interaction seems to be increasing exponentially. For our human minds, the result is we are pulled in many directions and pushed into many degrees of stress.

Humans are limited in the number of relationships and points of contact we can maintain – no matter how many friends, followers, and fans you may have.

In the 1990s -- eons before the explosion of social media options -- British anthropologist Robin Dunbar proposed that humans naturally and comfortably can maintain 150 stable relationships where we know who the person is and how the person relates to us. The theory is based on a correlation between primate brain size and average social group size. As Professor Dunbar wrote in his 1996 *Grooming, Gossip and the Evolution of Language*, "Putting it another way, it's the number of people you would not feel embarrassed about joining uninvited for a drink if you happened to bump into them in a bar."

One hundred-fifty became known as "Dunbar's number."

Twenty years later, Professor Dunbar published a new study in the journal *Royal Society Open Science*, and concluded the same limits apply to online relationships. Although "Dunbar's number" has its detractors, we know our ability to maintain relationships is limited.

Yet we have, through technology, created a system where almost every human can be over-committed all the time, putting everybody in a state of feeling stressed and overwhelmed.

On top of that, there are "the Joneses."

A New York Globe cartoon in 1913 inserted into our vocabulary an idiom for the desire to match one's neighbors in spending and social standing. There are studies, but we don't need them, to tell us that people disproportionately showcase their positive interactions and successes on social media while hiding their losses and disappointments. When we look around on social media, we see great things. We don't seem to be doing what everyone else is. We want to keep up with the Joneses.

We believe we are coming up short. This plays into our time management because when we are stressed, we cannot focus on our long-term direction. One of the fundamentals of time management is to deal with the pressures of stress.

To manage our time, we need to manage our stress.

For different people, different solutions.

A busy executive day-to-day and then week-to-week completely disconnects after a while. He steps away from business to commune with nature and others in a very holistic way on long hikes that last several days. Others set boundaries. She reserves times that she tries to not even think about work.

People build systems and processes that filter out what's unimportant. Business leaders at all levels cherish the gatekeepers who know what issues and which people to let through to the boss.

Misfits -- those who cannot help the organization in some way -- are a poor use of time.

The reality is that we have limited time and seemingly unlimited demands on us.

To be great, we need to manage our stress to be able to manage time, set priorities, and increase productivity.

4. Delegate

"I need to find more time."

We hear others say it. We say it. But let's not waste our time looking.

There are only 24 hours in a day. We can only do so much. We can only produce what we can do in the 168 we have in the week. We want to find more time? Sorry, we're unable to find that.

But we can make a more powerful use of our time, to use our time better so that, in a way, we create more time.

We can take control of our multitasking to be more effective. We can apply filters to make sure we work only on what's important. We can determine where to focus our time and attention – that is the most critical element of great productivity and time management.

One of this book's authors, R. Shawn McBride, calls the concept "captured power." Put all your strength into one area or endeavor in your business life, and you become great at it. That core activity is how you make your earnings and profits to fuel the rest of your business. And if you're not a business owner, your "captured power" is what makes you valuable to others.

The concept can be applied to creating productivity and growth for you as a manager or business executive. Accept the fact: None of us can do everything. As much as we may want to, we cannot tackle every task. This is good because it forces us to think about what we want to do, how we want to spend our 168 hours this week, and who we really are. It forces us to be part of a team. We work with those around us to make sure we accomplish what we need to, and that we let others participate and accomplish what they want.

There's something rewarding about how our limited time forces us to join teams.

People may assemble cars from kits or use components to build hot rods, and we may say the cars were built from scratch. But not really. Did the person dredge the iron ore, refine it, clean it in a coke furnace, shape the brake rotors and pads and engine components, then put it all together into a car? Some people say it's impossible for one person today to accomplish almost anything alone. We all rely on each other. No one could build a laptop computer alone – or know how. One person cannot manufacture every part. Plastic is needed for the keyboard. Screen technology. Hard drive. Microprocessor. The knowledge and logistics behind each component of the computer exceed more than one person's capability. We could probably say the same of a car, or perhaps even a pencil.

To find more time, find your focus. Know what makes you uniquely you, why you do what you do, and what you want to concentrate on. Then you can effectively delegate and involve others who will help you achieve greatness.

Some people hesitate – refuse, even – to delegate. Maybe they don't trust others with the task, or maybe they don't see themselves in a position to delegate. But in most cases, there are opportunities to focus and grow. It is likely that we all complete tasks that are very low value-added and are right for delegation.

How many of us open our mail, do our filing, and spend some of those 168 hours on tasks that may not be the highest and best use of our time?

For employees who work for an organization, it may be difficult to get the resources to delegate effectively. But it is worth trying as you build your career. You may be better off to accept resources to delegate instead of a pay raise because if you improve your focus and productivity, you will do so much more for the long-term plan than the incremental pay increases.

Take the long view. Think about how you can do what you are great at and truly enjoy. Then eliminate or delegate the tasks that you aren't great at or you don't enjoy. This will help you excel at what you do and be more productive overall. You cannot find the time, but you can be more productive with the time you have.

5. Dream

It may seem strange for a book about time management to encourage you to figure out your long-term visions and dreams. But don't be confused.

Everything is about priorities.

When we have a clear vision of where we want to be in the future, we learn what's important to us. We learn what needs to be worked on, and what doesn't. If we are to manage our time and set our priorities, we first need to make certain we know our destination.

We need that clear vision for the future.

Many people dislike planning. They find it boring. Or they find it pointless because they believe things will change. Not every plan works out the way it was intended. Perhaps none do.

But that's not the point.

By sitting down and thinking about where we want to go and what we want to attain, we set a clear direction on what's important and what's not. It becomes part of the decision-making process.

To start, consider Shawn McBride's vision-making process so that the focus and energy are in the right place.

It's really simple.

Determine where you are. Then dream. How do we want life to look? Where do we want to be at the end?

Relate that dream to steps. Now that we know where we are and where we want to be, we need to consider the natural and probable steps that will get us from here to there.

Evaluate the changes we need to make to get where we want to be. What needs to happen? Often the evaluation calls for fundamental changes. New skills. New training. New staffing within an organization. If we had the capabilities and were delivering the value we needed to be where we want to be, we could already be there. Build that process.

Adjust the plan. Once we start drafting the plan, we will find that not everything fits together the way we thought it would. Maybe the timelines were unrealistic, the steps weren't quite right, or we didn't need the changes we believed we did. Make adjustments before initiating the plan.

Modify the plan. We adjusted the plan during the planning stage. But as we begin to execute the plan to get where we want to go, the unexpected will happen. At this point, we modify the plan so it is updated and reworked through the dream process.

This is a simple way to envision your future, plot the path there, and act on it.

It should be clear that any discussion of time management depends on knowing where you want to go.

6. Filter

Open your email and watch the bombardment. *A revolutionary fitness plan builds muscle in just days! An amazing new pill staves off aging! A sure-fire software eliminates spam!* And that may be just the tip of the inbox iceberg.

There's no shortage of opportunity to spend your time and money in this world. And that can be a difficult thing to handle.

Successful people know they cannot do everything. They determine what they will do and what they won't. You know that. You know you must determine how you will and won't spend your time. Of course, that's easier said than done, especially with complex, interlocking relationships and competing demands with uncertain outcomes.

But you're on your way. You're dreaming about your future. You know where you want to go and what you want to do. At this point, with your dreams and visions as your compass, we can evaluate whether and how opportunities fit into your plan.

Many times, an opportunity will not have any connection to the dream so it can be eliminated almost immediately. (You don't need to check out the new car sale.) There is no need to spend time or energy on an opportunity that doesn't fit with your long-term vision.

Other opportunities may be trickier to evaluate. Some may have tangential connections to your dream but not be directly related. (Maybe you should look into the benefits of a new credit card offering.)

Some may clearly line up with your visions and dreams. (With your twins in kindergarten, it's time to talk with a financial advisor about

saving for college.) These opportunities will be the steps to take next to get where you want to be. Say "yes" to these opportunities.

Now we can sort opportunities because we evaluate everything based on our visions and dreams. Does the opportunity push us closer to our dream or pull us back? We adjust our process based on what we learn as we go. It's that simple. You now have a filter. Use it to save yourself from wasting time evaluating opportunities as they come to you – whether through unsolicited email, well-meaning colleagues, network acquaintances or the many other ways opportunities compete for your attention.

This is a positive thing. It is freeing up time for you.

7. Prioritize

This is a permission slip.

You are permitted to eliminate from your precious hours all that is inconsistent with your visions and dreams. Say good-bye to tasks you've taken on and now realize aren't getting you anywhere. Reject opportunities that are a misfit. Don't give in to pressure. This permission slip allows you to make choices guilt-free and without punishment. Free yourself up to execute on the things that you believe in and love.

Because now is the critical time to set priorities. For many, the process of deciding what is important frees up a lot of time.

Did you ever have a time as an adolescent when friends pressured you to do something you didn't want to do? It didn't necessarily have to be something that would get you detention or grounded if you got caught, but you didn't want to do it. So, you said, "My mom won't let me." That's not an option now.

But if you want one, feel free to cite this book's authors as the reason you cannot do something.

Tell whoever is pressuring you that we told you to say, "No." We will accept calls and emails for verification. After all, the authors are accustomed to being the bad guys and taking the flak. You are free to tell others that you will not help them, that you're unable to do more for them, and that they need to do things on their own because you're living your life based on your priorities.

1. Although you may feel bad about saying no to those people and opportunities not in line with your priorities, consider all the people who are important and all the opportunities that are worthwhile. Yo

will have more time to spend with the important people in your life. You will have more time to complete critical functions. You will have more time to help others of your choosing.

It's a paradox, but sometimes you get more done by doing less. You accomplish more in certain areas of life if you accomplish less in other areas. You will get more accomplished by setting your priorities and sticking to them.

2. The ability to delegate is key to successful time management. In this context, ability has two meanings: Are you psychologically able to let others take on the tasks that aren't your strengths and are you financially in a position that allows you to be able to assign others tasks that aren't the best use of your time? As you become more wealthy or secure higher positions in the business hierarchy, you will get more and more support.

Always think about delegation.

You know the things that are not your favorites or your strengths. Move these things off your plate, and you will be better able to build greater energy and focus on your priorities. Flex your delegation muscle in your business and personal life.

What in your personal life saps your energy and zaps your time? What on the personal side keeps you from accomplishments on the business side?

What about the other way? What can you turn over to others that will free you to do more of what you want on the personal side?

Assess all the routine day-to-day issues and get them delegated to people who can handle them competently. This will allow you to execute your priorities and the more creative and out-of-the-routine opportunities with high value.

3. Focus on your priorities. Remind yourself often of what is next in your plan. Audit, perhaps daily or weekly, to see how you spent your time and whether it was consistent with your priorities. The more often you review, the better you will know if you are devoting your time and energy to what's important.

4. Build your "No muscle." People often struggle to say no because it seems easier to say yes. One of the ways students score high marks in school is that they say yes to everything and do exactly what is expected of them. That usually works for a while, and then it's like hitting a wall. Because in the real world, in the business world, one person cannot accomplish everything. You must say "No" to projects that may have some potential, friends whose requests don't match your priorities and low-revenue clients. That gives you time for your higher priorities.

The more you say no the easier it will be for you to say it. When you're an expert at no you can work on your priorities, not other people's priorities.

8. Reset

Life can be messy.

Once you've determined your true dreams and evaluated your priorities, don't expect to coast.

What is important today may not be tomorrow. Values shift. Things don't always happen in the order we anticipate. And they certainly don't happen because we expect them. Breakthroughs may come on suddenly or incrementally. Projects may succeed or struggle.

That is life – at work and home. Your business partnership or marriage may fall apart over time as disagreements mount or values change, or you may be ambushed with the news that the other person wants out. Or the relationships may grow stronger over time, and you may find that together your priorities have changed or your dreams have evolved.

Go back. Reassess your dreams periodically. But constantly revisit your priorities to make sure your time and attention are in the right place.

9. Seek Help

Think of an athlete you consider "world-class."

No matter who comes to mind, two things are certain: Those at the top worked very hard and did not get there on their own.

The best athletes have a coach. The best athletes are accountable to others.

If cool-as-a-cucumber professional golfers, dominating beach volleyball players and pro basketball MVPs have coaches working with them to achieve their goals, why would business people be any different? Why wouldn't anyone who wants to excel not benefit from an expert's insight, counsel, and motivation?

You want someone on your team who has an outside perspective to help you accomplish all you want to do. But finding the right coach can be difficult – just look at the revolving-door life of athletic coaches at all levels.

To find a coach who will push you and develop you, ask successful people for references or advice on what worked for them. Look around your community and network to determine who might be an excellent coach for you. Search online. Read. Find people whose philosophies match yours.

Along with a coach – or instead of a coach if it is not financially feasible now – you also need to recruit an accountability buddy.

Recall the Dominican University study that demonstrated that writing down your goals improves your chances of reaching them.

It also found that those who are accountable to a supportive buddy and who check in with the buddy regularly are even more likely to see their goals become a reality. A lot of people in the business world would have known that was true without the study.

Your accountability buddy can be a business owner or executive who faces challenges similar to yours. Most people will go to the gym if they know a workout buddy or personal trainer is waiting for them. You probably can find someone who also is trying build the "No" muscle. Work with that buddy. Check in with each other periodically to make sure you both are doing what is most important for your long-term plan. As you cheer each other on, you will see each other get stronger. You may see huge gains in your ability to get things accomplished.

Build the team behind you. Get that coach. Get that accountability buddy. And, very importantly, make sure you work with people outside your company. You don't want to hang your dirty laundry at the office. You don't want everyone to know your struggles. Find people outside your home organization who can work with you and make sure you do the right things in the right order.

10. Get Comfortable

We'd all have defined abdominal muscles and toned arms if it were easy. Think of that when we say we need strong muscles to manage time, too.

The muscle to build and focus on your dreams. The muscle to delegate. The muscle to say no.

The muscles of time management don't develop overnight. It takes time to get comfortable with big visions and big dreams, and then more time to work toward them, and then more time to re-evaluate and reassess.

All the principles of time management and prioritization and productivity seem foreign at first. As you act on them more and more, they start to become more routine, more comfortable, and more something you want to do regularly. Build these muscles so you are strong and able to control your time.

11. Refine and Improve

One of the biggest obstacles to effective time management is the belief that there are limits to what people can do. People perceive they can do only so much in a given period. Often it is because of poor benchmarking.

People compare themselves to those around them, calculating that their capabilities must be similar. Imagine the unproductive co-worker who cannot complete assignments. Before long the office vibe is that no one can get all the work finished in the allotted time. Soon everyone falls behind. Everyone reinforces the belief that the work cannot be completed. Then a consultant or advisor from outside is brought in – someone not tainted by the office norms – and suddenly everyone is productive, and the work is finished on time.

Everyone steps up their game.

For years it was considered impossible for a human to run a mile in four minutes. The benchmark seemed unattainable. Then in May 1954, Roger Bannister ran a mile in 3 minutes 59.4 seconds. Poof. Everybody knew a four-minute mile was possible. Just 46 days later, Bannister's rival ran an even faster mile. Then more and more male runners were running miles in less than four minutes. Far less. In a half century, the record for a mile has dropped 17 seconds, and high school runners have broken the 4-minute benchmark. The limits were artificial.

We see the same phenomenon with time management and productivity: People believe there are preset limits on what humans can do and what is possible.

That's untrue.

We can each do more. We can manage our time and build the right systems and have the right focus. We need to know where we're going and how we're getting there. Time management is a journey and can be a key to your success. Refine and improve. Refine and improve. You will get there.

Part Two

PRODUCTIVITY

12. The Golden Triangle

If you've studied management, you likely know about Harold Leavitt. If not, it's time for a quick introduction.

Professor Leavitt was a pioneering psychologist of management who in 1965 demonstrated that the four elements in an organization -- people, goals and tasks, structure, and technology and processes -- are interdependent. Change in one impacts all. The four elements are the four points of what is called "Leavitt's Diamond," which is the model others have followed and built on in the last half century when analyzing change.

Our goal is to change, to manage time better and be more productive.

To that end, we turn to the "Golden Triangle" framework, which was based on "Leavitt's Diamond" and popularized in the 1980s as a method to drive business change. It can and should be applied for personal and even organizational productivity.

Any system -- for your own life or in your business -- should consider:

-- WHO is involved (the people)
-- WHAT will be affected (the process)
-- HOW it will be changed (the technology)

People, process and technology are the three points of the "Golden Triangle."

It's important to note that the triangle operates just like a three-legged stool; each leg depends on the others to derive its strength, and when one is shorter or even missing, the stool becomes inoperable. Once you've decided that you can manage your time better and become more productive, consider how the three primary components work together. If you decide to utilize a new technology, for example, but haven't considered how you'll change your process in light of the new technology, it is highly likely that the people will revolt and the technology will flounder.

You have probably experienced spurts of time when you are highly productive: It's the week before you leave for vacation and, being time-crunched with loads of personal and professional deliverables, you are able to get all of the laundry done, pack all the clothes and extras like beach chairs and beach towels, get the dogs off to the kennel, squeeze in a pedicure, throw away all of the perishable food in your refrigerator, get the oil changed in the car, complete that report your boss is waiting on, delegate your weekly tasks to your co-workers, clean your leftovers out of the office refrigerator, set your out-of-office email message, answer a batch of incoming emails, and deliver some information to your clients.

Phew! Does that sound like way more than a week's worth of work? And yet, you're able to squeeze it all in when there is a payoff. There are other times that you can be hyper-productive because of deadlines, or even because it's just a few weeks before the holidays and you've got to get gifts for teachers, hairdressers, security guards, and the other people you always put off until the last minute.

You can harness that power of productivity and apply it to both your personal and professional lives by measuring and applying the "Golden Triangle" of people, process, and technology.

13. People and Eagerness

As you read this for the first time, focus on only one of the many roles you have in life and an important change you have at hand.

You're a sales manager who needs your team to be more productive to meet this year's increased goal.

You're a coach who needs your players to be more productive in their downtime to increase their strength and flexibility.

You're a parent who needs to spend less time on household chores in order to be able to spend more time with family.

We begin to apply the "Golden Triangle" with people -- your co-workers, your employees, your friends, the non-profit board you volunteer for, even yourself. People are naturally resistant to change. It cannot be understated: Human beings prefer stasis, as it is dependable and it is what we know.

Everett Rogers, a communication theorist and sociologist, described the rate at which new technology, and along with it, new ideas, spread. In 1962, in his seminal work, *Diffusion of Innovations*, he found that less than 16% of the population falls into the categories of "innovators" and "early adopters." This is significant because as you plan to launch a new process or technology, you must consider the human factor and response. *"That's the way we've always done it"* is a pervasive statement that is expressed both during times of change and times of stasis.

So, how can you get the people amped up for your new methods of productivity?

First, start with the *WIIFM*; people always want to know "What's in it for me?" As you hone in on the new, more productive methods, you should also outline what cause and effect will have the most positive impact on the people in your situation. Even if the "people" is just yourself, knowing the benefits allows you to continue to push for that reward, even if the new method challenges your balance.

On this first read, you have focused on a most pressing issue. Once you have that in place, come back and read it again to apply the process to the other areas of your life that could use freshening. No one wants to be Kodak or Blockbuster. Change is good when it causes innovation.

14. Process and Efficiency

Which came first: The chicken or the egg? The process and technology elements of our triangle are a bit like that. Your process may depend on your technology, but your technology should enhance -- not replace -- your process. It's a causality dilemma.

So why aren't you productive?

A great way to tease out a root cause is the "Five Whys" exercise, created by Taiichi Ohno, pioneer of the Toyota production system in the 1950s. He saw problems as opportunities in disguise. He encouraged his staff to ask "why" five times to get to the root of a problem, although not all problems have a single cause. The trick is to ask "why" until you get to a cause that can be solved. For example:

My team is not productive. WHY?

They are all generalists, but those with specialist experience get pulled into client projects that aren't theirs, leaving them less time to work on assigned deliverables. WHY?

When we added full-time headcount, we didn't separate the jobs or job descriptions to take the specialist needs into account. WHY?

We didn't look at the "bigger picture" to set up our new headcount for scalability, and just tried to plug in warm bodies quickly. WHY?

Our department manager is inexperienced with scaling. WHY?

Our company is growing very quickly, and we are promoting from within, creating managers from individual contributors.

In this instance, you can trace the team's unproductivity to the "green" manager who doesn't yet know to step back and evaluate the bigger picture for scalability but instead rushes forward and hires many more people with the same job title and job description.

Once you identify a root of the issue, you can set up a process to help mitigate the risk.

Process is beneficial, as it gives predictable methods to perform the same tasks and the expectation of the same results. Think of your morning shower. You likely follow the same steps every time: shampoo, condition, wash face, wash body, rinse conditioner. This rote process allows you to carry out this task efficiently and effectively and is quite productive. Your goal is to create a process that attacks all of your rote tasks first, and then move to the dynamic, or non-rote tasks.

Process is best when it's written into a work instruction or standard operating procedure. This allows for quick reference when the process isn't routine, and for multiple people to perform tasks in a unified way. Think about any time you have walked into a Target store. It's likely that the departments were set up in the same order no matter the store's location, allowing for a unified experience for the customer. That's our goal here.

Be certain to date stamp all formal process documentation, and set yourself a calendar reminder to revisit the process -- monthly, quarterly, annually, or whatever time fits your specific process.

15. Technology and Effectiveness

Technology surrounds us. There's the connected home, the internet of things -- even the buzzwords are their own sort of technology! How can we, then, use technology to improve efficiency and therefore productivity?

One of our authors uses technology to run the household. For example, if she buys show tickets, it goes into the Google calendar. If she's traveling for work, the entire trip and details go into the calendar. If he has a weekend bike trip with his buddies, it goes into the Google calendar. This calendar is integrated into their smartphones, so there is always living, real-time documentation that shows the time demands. Mistakes are rare; the get-away isn't planned for the same weekend as a family birthday party. Using technology in this way -- changing the process away from a paper or chalkboard calendar -- allows for everyone in the family to be up-to-date at all times and minimizes uncertainty and doubt.

Once you've identified the issue that you're trying to solve, and used the Five Whys to get to a root cause, you can begin to nominate technology or automation that can solve your challenges. If you want to help an entire company automate back-office systems, you evaluate ERP (enterprise resource planning) platforms; if you want to batch your social media efforts, you evaluate social media scheduling tools.

Technology can be integrated into your life – again, professional or personal – but must take into consideration the people who need it, how to roll it out to them, and what process will need to be considered.

It's important to note that technology doesn't only mean an app on your phone or computer. Technology also could be used to describe the automation that can occur after evaluation of *how* you perform a task, such as single-piece flow or batching production. Will you pack your entire suitcase first, and then your child's? Or will you pack everyone's pajamas, then everyone's socks, and so on?

Conclusion

The world will continue to present you with obstacles and pressures on your time. As the globalization of communication and entertainment pushes forward, competition for your available productive time will increase.

Our hope is that you use this book as a reference. Pick it up when you feel time-crunched or overwhelmed, and work through what is actually being asked of you and how you can prioritize those demands.

Often, we speak of work and life balance; as an interconnected people, with smartphones and rapidly advancing technologies, the line between work and life will certainly continue to blur. You set your priorities: What will you spend your minutes on, and how can those minutes be as productive as possible?

Acknowledgments

I'd like to acknowledge my clients, friends and fellow authors who contributed to this book. I live time management -- running my businesses, helping my clients run their businesses, speaking to audiences and living my personal life. Time is the most valuable asset to be harnessed, used and managed. Others have taught me how.

To my team that supports projects like this and makes them reality by dotting I's and crossing T's while I lead the next project to grow my business, "Thank You." I know how much you contribute to what we are able to accomplish.

-- R. Shawn McBride

Taking a book from concept to reality in a matter of weeks seemed insane to me, but when Shawn proposed it, I figured there would be no better way to prove that we really understand how to be productive!

I'd like to thank my friends and family, all of whom pitched in to help this book come together, all of whom keep me entertained, and all of whom always support my efforts (as crazy as some of them may be -- truly!) I love you all so much. I cannot imagine my life without any of you.

-- Shannon J. Gregg

About the Authors

Shannon J. Gregg, MBA: Sales productivity expert. Sales tech geek. Sales operations fanatic. Salesforce obsessed.

Shannon is an aficionado of sales technology to increase efficiency in the sales process, and an early adopter and adoption influencer for sales technology systems, particularly Salesforce.com and technology that integrates with the Salesforce platform. She is a change agent, particularly in merger & acquisition environments (venture capital and private equity) with a successful record of integrating process, product/service pricing and pricing methodologies, and notably, global teams, with cultural sensitivity.

Having stood up three sales operations teams in technology firms, Shannon is no stranger to the needs of a growing company to identify efficient and effective sales processes in order to drive revenue as quickly as possible. She's hyper-focused on improving sales productivity and optimization, and is known for her ability to hone in on areas to improve with a lean approach. She's also known for her charismatic candor.

Shannon is a full-time head of business development operations. She provides keynote talks, consultation and workshops on sales productivity. Visit www.ShannonGregg.com for information and resources.

R. Shawn McBride loves planning. Crazy, huh?

Shawn started his career as a corporate lawyer helping people develop and protect their business plans. As his career evolved, Shawn became a trusted advisor on all aspects of planning. He now runs the R. Shawn McBride Law Firm and his business strategy firm, McBride for Business.

Shawn believes good plans are the key to move you from daydreaming to the life of your dreams.

With his passion for helping others build their dreams for themselves and their teams, Shawn works one-on-one with select clients and is a keynote speaker for large gatherings. He knows most people don't have plans or know where to begin planning. He possesses the expertise to help his clients, audiences, social media followers and readers design their plans. Books like this are one of the tools he creates to build successful strategies.

His website, www.McBrideForBusiness.com, is the place to start when you want to make things happen. He and his team will customize a plan for you. The website offers free resources for business owners, including a worksheet to maximize your business value.

When taking a break from McBride for Business and his law firm, www.McBrideAttorneys.com, Shawn enjoys the outdoors, history and antique cars.

Worksheet

Please use this worksheet to record your goals and notes as you read this book. This will help you to keep track of your thoughts, and serve as a record for you to check back on your progress on the path to time management and productivity.

Don't worry if you want to read the book a second, third, or tenth time -- this worksheet is available for free download at websites mcbrideforbusiness.com and shannongregg.com.

What are your visions and dreams? Track them here.

Dream _____

Relate_____

Evaluate_____

Adjust_____

Modifications _____

What are your priorities? List them here.

_____

_____

_____

What can you delegate? Brainstorm ideas here.

_____

_____

_____

Who could be your coach or accountability buddy? List some ideas.

_____

_____

_____

Who are the people you are trying to influence to improve?

_____

_____

What is the process that you are trying to improve?

_____

_____

The Five Whys: What issue are you facing?

_____

_____

Why?

_____

_____

Why?

_____

_____

Why?

_____

_____

Why?

_____

_____

Why?

_____

_____

What technology could you consider for your current "people" and "process?"

_____

_____